THE COMMON MAN'S FINANCIAL GUIDE

WORKBOOK

"Making Money Work for You"

Volume 1: Getting Started

E. Donell Smith

(Author of *The Common Man's Financial Guide*)

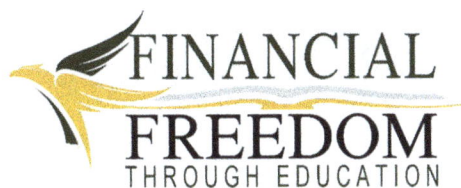

FINANCIAL
FREEDOM
THROUGH EDUCATION

Entegrity Choice Publishing
PO Box 453
Powder Springs, GA 30127
info@entegritypublishing.com
www.entegritypublishing.com
770.727.6517

Printed in the United States of America

Library of Congress Cataloging-in-Publication Data
ISBN 978-1-7330301-7-5

ENTEGRITY
CHOICE PUBLISHING

TABLE OF CONTENTS

UNDERSTAND *YOUR* RISK TOLERANCE

What is Risk Tolerance?

Definition: **Risk** takes on many forms but is broadly categorized as the chance an outcome or investment's actual return *will differ* from the expected outcome or return.

Definition: **Risk-averse** refers to investors who, when faced with two investments with a similar expected return, prefer the lower-risk option.

Definition: **Risk tolerance** *is the degree of <u>variability</u> in investment returns that an investor is willing to withstand in their <u>financial planning</u>. Risk tolerance is an important component in <u>investing</u>. You should have a realistic understanding of your ability and willingness to stomach large <u>swings</u> in the value of your investments; if you take on too much risk, you might panic and sell at the wrong time.* (Chen, 2018)

In order to really invest without being afraid or feeling that you are not equipped to trade stocks, you have to determine what is your tolerance for price movement. Because you have been taught or developed an aversion to losing money, any downward movement in the price of a stock you purchased may feel like you are losing. The exact opposite is true, if you remember from the Common Man's Financial Guide, the best time to buy any goods or service is when there has been "bad news" and you can purchase more shares at a lower price. This comfort begins with knowing that the company, that you are now an owner of, is here to stay. You stabilized this strategy by only buying companies that have a great history, are still needed in our society, and demonstrate great promise for future development and profits.

Reducing Risk Tolerance

The best way to reduce risk is to **only** buy companies that are proven, are found all over the world, are known to you, are game changers, innovate as tastes and interests change, and continue to operate with integrity. Never look at a reduction in price of these stocks (due to bad news) as a negative but as a positive. Since most of us have no choice but to purchase stocks over a long period of time (ten or more years), we actually need the price of the more expensive stocks to move downward on occasion to allow us to buy them at a discount!

Calculating Your Risk Tolerance

Take the following quiz to calculate your risk tolerance; that will help you determine which type of companies to purchase. A company with a high variable in its stock price is considered by the industry to be riskier than a stock whose price moves in a more consistent manner. This is a personal preference that only you and/or your spouse can determine.

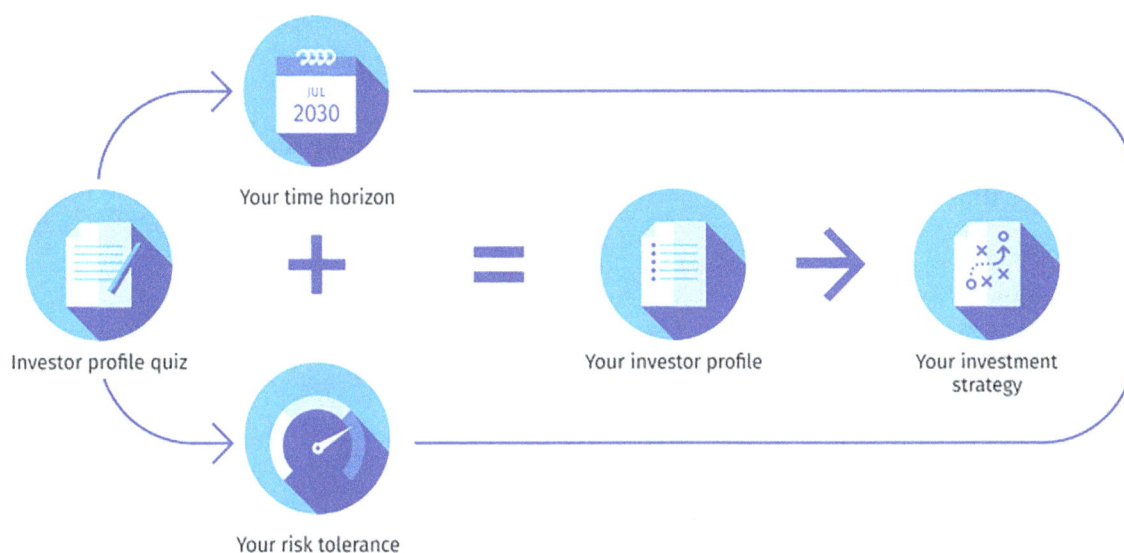

Image reprinted from Charles Schwab.com

10 Must-Have Questions in Risk Tolerance Questionnaire

Instructions: For each question, circle the number that corresponds to your best answer, and add them up. (Your spouse should answer independently.)

A. Investment Objectives

The purpose of this section is to help you understand your own idea of risk and if you are willing to take greater risks for a greater chance of increased rewards. Unless you are sure about the risk you want to take, you will not be able to plan, nor will you be able to work your plan.

a. What is your investment attitude?

1. Very conservative
2. Somewhat conservative
3. Moderate
4. Somewhat aggressive
5. Very aggressive

b. **In how many years will you begin making withdrawals from your investment?**

1. Less than a year
2. 1-2 years
3. 3-5 years
4. 6-9 years
5. 10-15 years
6. 15-25 years
7. More than 25 years

c. **Once you begin making withdrawals, how many years will you be making withdrawals?**

1. Lump-sum
2. 1-2 years
3. 3-5 years
4. 6-9 years
5. 10-15 years
6. 15-25 years
7. More than 25 years

B. Risk Tolerance

Investment decisions are usually determined by risk taken against the returns received. Risk is defined as possibly any loss to your portfolio or investment. To understand this, the following set of questions need to be asked:

d. Protecting my portfolio is more important to me than high returns.

1. Strongly agree
2. Agree
3. Neutral
4. Disagree
5. Strongly disagree

e. Keeping the above answer option in mind, which of the following statements make the most sense to you?

1. I am more interested in something to completely avoid losses.
2. I am concerned about losses along with returns.
3. I am willing to bear the consequences of a loss to maximize my returns.

f. Which of the following statements best describes your investment philosophy?

1. I feel comfortable with stable investments.

2. I am willing to withstand some fluctuations in my investmen.t

3. I am seeking substantial investment returns.

4. I am seeking potentially high investment returns.

g. **What do you expect to be your next major expenditure?**

1. Buying a house

2. Paying college tuition

3. Capitalizing a new business venture

4. Providing for my retirement

h. **Over the next few years, you expect your annual income to:**

1. Stay the same

2. Grow moderately

3. Grow substantially

4. Decrease moderately

5. Decrease substantially

i. **Assuming that you want to invest in stocks, which one would you choose?**

1. Companies with significant technological advancement but selling their stocks at a low price.

2. Established well-known companies that have a potentially high rate of growth.

3. "Blue chip" stocks that pay the dividend.

4. Cutting edge companies that are new and innovative.

j. **Select the investment you currently have**

1. Bonds and/or funds

2. Others (ETFs, Mutual Funds, Index Funds, etc.)

3. Stocks of individual companies

4. FOREX, Crypto-currency

a.___b.___c.___d.___e.___f.___g.___h.___i.___j.___ Total_____ (Circle below)

Conservative Risk 10-20 … Moderate Risk 20-35 … Aggressive Risk 35-48

This is your current tolerance for risk.

Breaking Down Risk Tolerance

Risk tolerance assessments for investors abound, including risk-related surveys or questionnaires. As an investor, you may also want to review historical worst-case returns for different asset classes to get an idea of how much money you would feel comfortable losing if your investments have a bad year or series of bad years. Other factors affecting risk tolerance are the time horizon you have to invest, your future earning capacity, and the presence of other assets such as a home, pension, Social Security, or an inheritance. In general, you can take greater risk with investable assets when you have other, more stable sources of funds available. (Chen, 2018)

Consider yourself to have *Aggressive Risk* Tolerance if:

You are market-savvy. You have a deep understanding of securities and their propensities, allowing such individuals and institutional investors to purchase highly volatile instruments, such as small-company stocks that can plummet to zero or options' contracts that can expire worthlessly. While maintaining a base of riskless securities, aggressive investors reach for maximum returns with maximum risk.

Consider yourself to have *Moderate Risk* Tolerance if:

You can accept some risk to your principal investment but you want a balanced approach with intermediate-term time horizons of five to ten years. You want a combined large-company mutual funds with less volatile bonds and riskless securities; moderate investors often pursue a 50/50 structure. You may decide to adopt a typical strategy that involves investing half of your portfolio in a dividend-paying, growth fund.

Consider yourself to have *Conservative Risk Tolerance* if:

Conservative investors are willing to accept little, to no, volatility in their investment portfolios. Often, retirees who have spent decades building a nest egg are unwilling to allow any type of risk to their principal. A conservative investor targets vehicles that are guaranteed and highly liquid. Risk-averse individuals opt for bank certificates of deposit (CDs), money markets, or U.S. Treasuries for income and preservation of capital.

- NOTES / QUESTIONS-

DETERMINE YOUR FINANCIAL GOALS

It is imperative to know and understand your financial goals. The goals you set are as varied and different as the people who set them. It could be as simple as: a) have enough money to pay for college for two children, b) be able to retire with the same level of income as your working years, c) be able to retire debt-free and with enough money in the bank to travel the world, and d) be able to retire to a small quiet community and live comfortably on social security benefits along with Medicare/Medicaid. On the other hand, financial goals could be as lavish as owning several homes, boats, cars, and expensive things with access to tens of millions of dollars at your disposal.

Here are nine examples of smaller financial goals (milestones) that you can consider setting for yourself on your way to the future:

1. *Make a budget and live by it...*
2. *Pay off credit card debt...*
3. *Save an emergency fund...*
4. *Save for retirement...*
5. *Live below your means...*
6. *Develop skills to improve your income...*
7. *Save for your children's education...*
8. *Save a down payment for a home...*
9. *Improve your credit score...*

This step in the financial process gives you the chance to dream, and plan for your future, and that of your immediate family as well as the generations to come. Some financial goals include setting aside funds for children, grandchildren, and the care of elderly family members. Other goals include paying off revolving debts such as credit cards and department store accounts. It could also mean creating and funding an emergency fund. Some of your goals will be short-term in nature while others will have a longer time horizon. In either case, goals need to have the following things in common:

1) Goals have to be specific.
2) Goals have to be measurable.
3) Goals must be action-oriented.
4) Goals need to be realistic, and
5) Goals have to be outlined with appropriate milestones to measure progress.

FINANCIAL GOALS CHART

GOAL	IS IT MEASURABLE?	ACTIONS NEEDED	IS THE GOAL REALISTIC?	SPECIFIC MILESTONES

Use the table above/below to get started recording your personal, family, or business (s) financial goals.

GOAL	IS IT MEASURABLE?	ACTIONS NEEDED	IS THE GOAL REALISTIC?	SPECIFIC MILESTONES

After filling in the table, it is imperative to re-visit your goals every six months to measure, update, and revise your initial assessment. It should be your goal to make the appropriate adjustments in order to ensure the success of reaching your intended goals. Some of your goals will change as you go through the process and some will be dropped/added as necessary as your desires and dreams change.

- NOTES / QUESTIONS-

GETTING STARTED

Setting Up Your Trading Account

Several companies offer trading platforms for beginners to the super advanced. Most trading sites are easy to use but they all have different tools to aid you. Here are a few of the online trading platforms that can assist you reach some of your goals:

Best Online Brokers for Beginner Stock Traders

- **TD Ameritrade** - *Best overall for beginners, but some tools are difficult to use.*
- **Fidelity** - *Great for education and research.*
- **E*TRADE** - *Best web-based platform that is simple and easy to use.*
- **Charles Schwab** - *Well-rounded site that has all the tools from beginner to advanced.*
- **Robinhood** - *Easy to use but no available tools.*
- **Acorns** – *Uses your spare change to invest but management fees are high for small accounts.*

The best place to trade for all levels has traditionally been **Charles Schwab.** Account *setup is free and all online trades are free.* It has all the tools needed to help the novice or to assist the savviest of professional traders. Most of the sites and apps above are easy enough to use, but the layout of the Schwab platform is the easiest to understand, to navigate, and to apply the lessons learned concerning stocks, bonds, ETFs, Mutual Funds, options, and precious metals.

Setting up your Schwab Account

a. Go to Schwab.com
b. Select "Accounts"
c. For a qualified account select "Traditional IRA" account, or
d. For an emergency fund account, select "Brokerage Account."
e. Choose if the account will be "individual" or "joint" with a spouse.
f. Enter your personal information and answer all the investment questions.
g. **Do not choose** the "**margin account**" option as it is for the most advanced.
h. Select the option to connect your Schwab and bank account.
i. You will need to have your bank logon and password information available.
j. After your accounts are linked you will be able to transfer funds easily.

Selecting Which Stocks to Buy

In the *Common Man's Financial Guide* choosing which companies to invest in is based on common everyday companies that you, your family, friends, and neighbors use their products and or services. List the places where you shop and buy your goods and services. The companies you select should be great companies that have the potential to withstand the highs and lows of economic challenges and create calm out of chaos. (Smith, 2019)

List of Your Top 20 Companies

Company Name	Stock Symbol	Price per Share	Number of Shares	Total Cost	Date

The best companies are all over the world and their products are part of the very fabric of every society. All you have to do, is think of those companies you, your families, and friends use on a routine basis and frankly don't think you can do without. Here are some *examples* of the type of companies you may want to list: Nike, McDonald's, Apple, Coke, Walmart, Home Depot, Star Bucks, Pizza Hut, Kentucky Fried Chicken, Netflix, Google, Visa, Intuit, Tesla, Lockheed Martin, Beyond Meat, Lowes, Federal Express, QualCom, Uber, Spotify, Paycom, Auto Zone, Bank of America, Toyota, and Disney, just to name a few.

Get with the members of your family, select as many companies as you can think of that you use or feel that you cannot do without! Before putting the stocks in the chart, rank them in order from 1-20, and then enter them into the chart.

Select the top five companies on your list and if you can, buy 1-10 shares of these five first. As an **example**, here is Visa from the Schwab website:

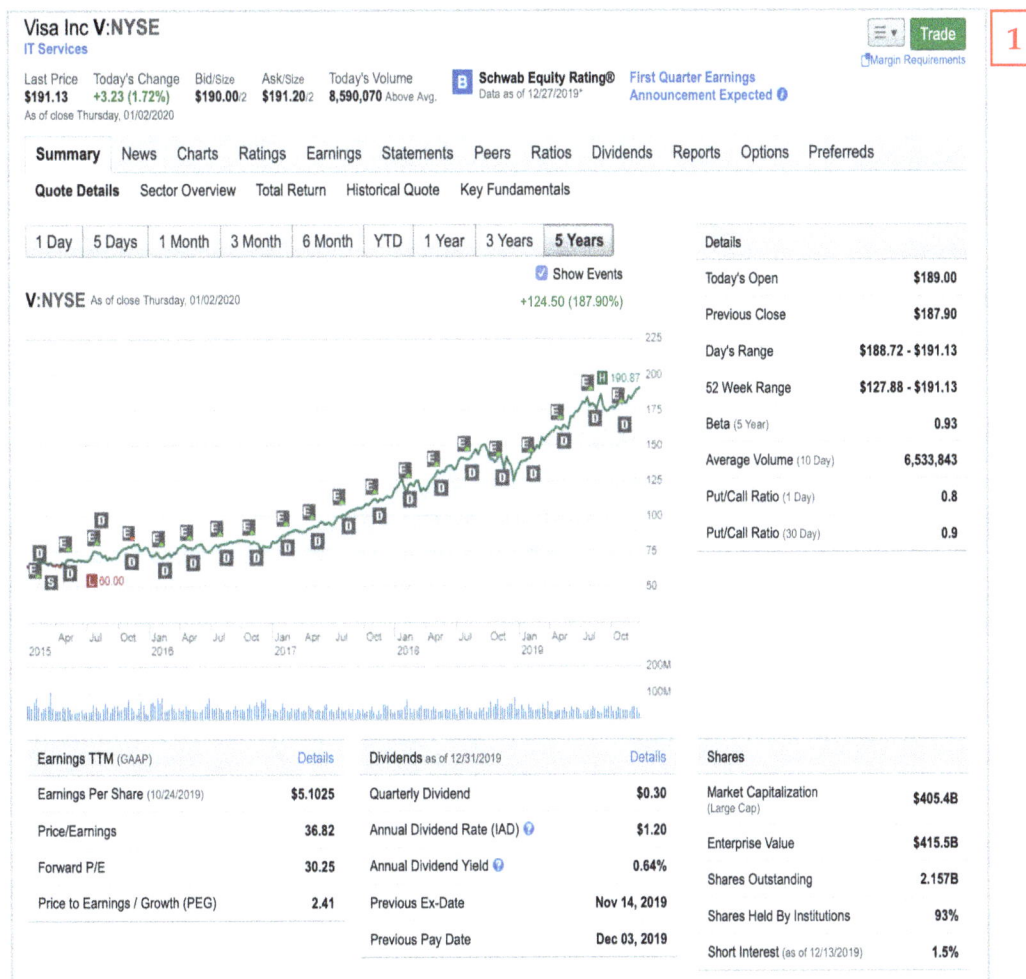

Reprinted from Schwab.com (DJIA, 2020)

To purchase the stock:

1. Click on the green "Trade" block. `1`
2. Select "Buy" from the 'action' drop-down menu. `2`
3. Enter the number of shares you want to buy, or use the calculator to enter the amount of money you want to spend (and it will calculate the number of shares). `3`

4. Select "re-invest" dividends and "market order". `4`

5. The final two steps are *"Review Order"* and *"Submit Order."* `5`

(Visa Trade, 2020)

- NOTES / QUESTIONS-

REMEMBER THE RULE OF '72

The Rule of 72 has been a common concept and financial tool for many years, simply used to calculate a rough estimate of how long it takes an investment to double in value based on the average rate of return. For example, if you invest in a guaranteed government bond at 4.5 percent interest, based on the rule, it would take approximately 16 years to double.

$$\frac{72}{\text{Rate of Return}} = \text{Time for Investment to Double}$$

This formula is useful because it simplifies the math for different investment vehicles you may have the option to choose from. Investment tools include individual stocks, mutual funds, exchange traded funds (ETFs), index funds, target date funds, corporate bonds, government bonds, municipal bonds, foreign exchange, and crypto currencies, just to name a few. Each of these investment vehicles come with its own set of rules, risks, language, tax implications, and levels of return. It is important to note that this workbook only gives you the basics in order to get you started on your financial journey.

The chart below gives you an idea how the concept works:

Interest Rate	Years to Double
1%	72
2%	36
3%	24
4%	18
5%	14
6%	12
7%	10.3
8%	9
9%	8
10%	7.2
11%	6.5
12%	6
13%	5.5
14%	5.1
15%	4.8

(Rule of 72, 2020)

Use the *worksheet* below to fill in your current return on investment and calculate how long it's going to take for your investments to double. Each investment you own will have a different return on investment (ROI).

Name of Investment	Basis		ROI		# of Years to Double
ex-Government Bond	72	÷	4.5%	=	16 years
Visa (10-yr avg)	72	÷	29%	=	2.48 years
	72	÷		=	
	72	÷		=	
	72	÷		=	
	72	÷		=	
	72	÷		=	

The type of investment you choose will be influenced by your individual risk tolerance, your time available, and your understanding of the investment chosen. This is just the beginning. As you get excited and begin to understand more, you may want to read more books on the subject that are listed in *The Common Man's Financial Guide*. In the meantime, get started by figuring out what to buy and what an average ROI will be for your chosen investment.

- NOTES / QUESTIONS-

COMPOUND INTEREST

Compound interest can work in your favor, or it can work against you. According to Albert Einstein, *"He who understands it, **earns it**, but he who doesn't, **pays it**!"* If you have ever purchased a home using a 30-year mortgage you may have seen a line on the paperwork showing the:

Amount Borrowed	–	$250,000.00
Interest Rate (APR)	–	5.5% (6.81%)
Monthly Payment	–	$1,419.47
Total Interest Paid	–	**$261,011.49**
Total Payment	–	**$511,011.49**

After 30 years of mortgage payments the total payments equal twice the amount of the original mortgage. <u>Wow, that's compound interest working against you!</u>

How do you get compound interest to ***work for you***? How do you know that certain investments will deliver great returns year after year after year?

1. You <u>must</u> *pick great companies*, great mutual funds, great index funds, or great dividend stocks, etc.

2. *Check the historical charts* to see how the entities performed over the past 1, 5, and 10 years.

3. Try to *decide* if the companies you choose will be ***relevant in the future*** and for what period. For example, most if not all smartphones will have to be replaced in order to use the up and coming 5G network. If these phones must be replaced, then those providers of smartphones, LG, Apple, Samsung, etc. will have to sell new phones in order to retain market share of the smartphone industry. This push into the new technology will cause all companies associated with it (5G) to have the potential to grow and expand.

4. Try to purchase the investments when you hear ***"bad news"*** that is news that may cause your company or investment to go "on sale." Or, you see a sharp dip in the price of a great company, and you surmise that it is temporary; creating a buying opportunity.

5. Check the following chart for Apple (AAPL) and Starbucks (SBUX) and circle the areas when the stock price decreased such, that you would consider purchasing more shares.

AAPL Apple Inc.

299.80 +2.37 **299.33** -0.47
At Close   After Hours

1M   3M   6M   1Y   2Y   5Y   **10Y**

305
234
164
93

2010   2012   2014   2016   2018

Great time to buy!

SBUX Starbucks Corporation

88.13 -0.70 **88.13** +0.00
At Close   After Hours

1M   3M   6M   1Y   2Y   5Y   **10Y**

101
78
55
32

2010   2012   2014   2016   2018

Great time to buy!

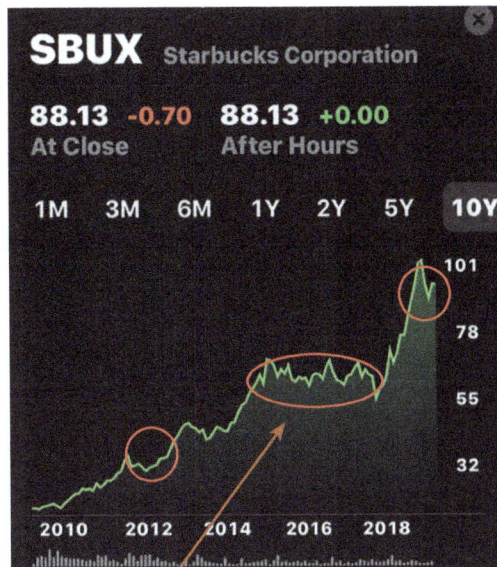

Most people are wired to sell their shares when the price drops a significant amount. According to Warren Buffett, you must be brave when others are afraid. Selling your shares at the wrong time can cause you to miss out on a dividend payment. Check the company's chart on the Schwab website to find the exact date the board of directors of the company is planning to issue a dividend. Just waiting a few days could be the difference between a few percent of return (i.e. compound interest) and taking a lost on your initial investment.

Microsoft Corp MSFT:NASDAQ
Software

Last Price	Today's Change	Bid/Size	Ask/Size	Today's Volume	Schwab Equity Rating®	Second Quarter Earnings
$159.03	+0.41 (0.26%)	$158.68/1	$158.70/4	20,815,370 Average	Data as of 01/03/2020*	Announcement Expected

As of close Monday, 01/06/2020

Summary   News   Charts   Ratings   Earnings   Statements   Peers   Ratios   Dividends   Reports   Options   Preferreds

Quote Details   Sector Overview   Total Return   Historical Quote   Key Fundamentals

1 Day | 5 Days | 1 Month | 3 Month | 6 Month | YTD | 1 Year | 3 Years | **5 Years**

MSFT:NASDAQ As of close Monday, 01/06/2020

☑ Show Events
+111.84 (237.00%)

H 160.73

L 39.72

Apr | Jul | Oct | Jan | Apr | Jul | Oct | Jan | Apr | Jul | Oct | Jan | Apr | Jul | Oct | Jan | Apr | Jul | Oct | Jan
2015 | 2016 | 2017 | 2018 | 2019 | 2020

Details

Today's Open	$157.08
Previous Close	$158.62
Day's Range	$156.51 - $159.10
52 Week Range	$100.98 - $160.73
Beta (5 Year)	1.17
Average Volume (10 Day)	21,539,775
Put/Call Ratio (1 Day)	0.6
Put/Call Ratio (30 Day)	0.5

The Quarterly dividend is $0.51 per share that you own!

Earnings TTM (GAAP)	Details		Dividends as of 01/03/2020	Details
Earnings Per Share (10/23/2019)	$4.9953		Quarterly Dividend	$0.51
Price/Earnings	31.75		Annual Dividend Rate (IAD)	$2.04
Forward P/E	26.15		Annual Dividend Yield	1.29%
Price to Earnings / Growth (PEG)	2.19		Next Ex-Date	Feb 19, 2020
			Next Pay Date	Mar 12, 2020

Microsoft will pay its next dividend on March 12th

Shares	
Market Capitalization (Large Cap)	$1.2T
Enterprise Value	$1.2T
Shares Outstanding	7.629B
Shares Held By Institutions	72%
Short Interest (as of 12/15/2019)	0.8%

(Microsoft Chart, 2020)

Microsoft's chart shows March 12, 2020 as the next pay day and in order to receive the dividend, you must own the stock by February 19, 2020 (next ex-date).

The *ex-dividend date* is the date that determines which shareholders will be entitled to receive the dividend. Typically, the *ex-dividend date* is set two business days before the record date (a snapshot of all shareholders on a particular business day). Only shareholders who owned their shares at least *two full business days* before the record date will be entitled to receive the dividend.

So, the overall goal is to constantly increase the number of shares you own overtime and allow the power of compound interest to work in your favor. As you gain more and more shares the number of dividends you receive or re-invest will also increase until the compounding effect begins to grow exponentially. Dividends work for you as they are now helping the overall value of your investment to increase. Now, your money is working for you!

Although you may have seen this example, it's always good to work the numbers yourself to reinforce the concept of interest. This example shows how compound interest can grow 1 into greater than $1 million in less than 30 days. It starts out small, but when the compounding hits exponential growth the results are astounding. Finish filling in the following matrix to show how $0.01 will grow by 100% each day for only 30 days.

.01 x 2 = .02	.02 x 2 = .04	.04 x 2 = .08	.08 x 2 = .16	.16 x 2 = .32
.32 x 2 = .64	.64 x 2 =			

Day 30 results = $_____

It's amazing what the power of compounding can do!

- NOTES / QUESTIONS-

THINGS YOU BUY AND USE

This is the fun part of *The Common Man's Financial Guide Workbook.* If you had any trouble picking twenty major companies, please list the most significant products and services you, and your family purchase on a daily, weekly, or monthly basis. It could be as simple as the type of toothpaste you love, to the name of the coffee you drink, to the car you drive, or the perfume you like the most. Think of the brand of shoes you love, to the place where you buy your hardware supplies, to the different brand of cereals you eat, and list all the places where you buy clothes. You can also list your cable provider, utility company, home builder, and telephone provider. So, spend a little time on this list and you will be surprised as to all the different areas in which you will find an investment opportunity!

Memory Jogger Charts: Use the headings below to jog your memory and enter the corresponding companies into the spaces in each column.

Memory Jogger Charts

Shoes and Clothes	Utility and Services	Miscellaneous	Hardware and Fuel

Grocery	Jewelry	Soap	Lotions	Vehicles	Electronics

Retirement	Perfume	Fast Food	Restaurants	Vehicles	Electronics

Fitness	Air Travel	Vacation	Hotels	Music	Toys

Compare this list with your top twenty companies that you listed in the previous section and add to that list as you find other great companies. Any time you need to make additional purchases or add to your investment portfolio, this list will be a great place to start looking for new companies.

- NOTES / QUESTIONS-

PURCHASE YOUR FIRST FIVE COMPANIES (INVESTMENTS/STOCKS)

Once you have secured your list of at least twenty stocks, it's time to buy a few shares of the companies you have rank ordered. It's important to keep in mind the idea to buy the investment on bad news, if you have the opportunity. Market volatility (the ups and downs of stock prices) will give opportunity to purchase one or several shares of different investments at a discount (*bad news*).

Top 5 Purchase Chart

Name of Company or Fund	Symbol	Price per Share	Number of Shares	Total Cost	Date Purchased

- NOTES / QUESTIONS -

ONE VERSUS THE OTHER

Some companies are in the same industry or provide similar services. Please *circle* the company that you and your family patronize the most. If you are not sure what it is, do a google search or a search on Schwab.com, on the company (symbol).

McDonald's versus Wendy's

Lowe's versus Home Depot

Visa versus Mastercard

Nike versus Adidas

Apple versus Dell

Lockheed Martin versus Northrop Grumman

Estée Lauder versus Revlon

Apple versus Samsung

Netflix versus Disney

Amazon versus Alibaba

SPY (S&P 500 index fund) versus QQQ (NASDQ index fund)

Lyft versus Uber

Federal Express versus United Parcel Service

Paycom Software versus Automatic Data Processing

Exxon Mobile versus British Petroleum

Bank of America versus JP Morgan

Coke versus Pepsi

Macy's versus Dillard's

CVS versus Walgreens

Toyota versus Mercedes Benz

Proctor and Gamble versus General Mills

Make You Own List of *Either/Or* Companies

_____ versus _____

_____ versus _____

_____ versus _____

_____ versus _____

_____ versus _____

_____ versus _____

_____ versus _____

- NOTES / QUESTIONS-

CALCULATING THE RETURN ON INVESTMENT (ROI)

ROI Formula

$$ROI = \left(\frac{\text{Gain From Investment} - \text{Cost Of Investment}}{\text{Cost Of Investment}} \right) \times 100$$

(Return on Investment)

What does it mean?

Gain from investment: Refers to your net income or profit for the year
Cost of Investment: Refers to the total amount you invested

Template.net

(Return on Investment, 2020)

It's important to know how to determine your return on investment to decide if your strategy is working. A few months after purchasing an investment you can use the above formula to find out your ROI for the number of months that you hold it (typically 12 months). If you are using Schwab.com the percent gain and/or loss will be displayed in the *"Gain/Loss"* column on your **positions** page.

For instance, if you purchased stock XYZ for $100 and on December 31st, 2018 the same stock is now (December 31, 2019) priced at $135 (difference of $35) your ROI is:

ROI = (135-100)/100 x 100 = 35/100 x 100 = $\boxed{\text{35\% per year}}$

On the other hand, if stock QRS is purchased at $1664 per share and one year later it is trading at $1798 (difference of $134) per share, your ROI is:

ROI = (1798-1664)/1664 x 100 = $\boxed{\text{8.05\% per year}}$

This shows that although stock QRS gained $134 (1798-1664), almost $100 more than stock XYZ, *XYZ had the greater ROI*.

The percent return ties back into the Rule of '72 which means your money will double every 2.06 years, and for QRS, it will take 8.94 years to double if the current trend continues.

Exercise: **Calculate ROI for the following investment.**

Stock purchased date: January 4, 2019

Stock price: $34.77

Sell date: December 28, 2019

Sell price: $49.53

Return on Investment: ☐

Stock purchase date: March 14, 2018

Stock price: $134.89

Sell date: March 13, 2019

Sell price: $107.36

Return on Investment: ☐

(If the value of your investment falls during the period, the ROI will be negative.)

- NOTES / QUESTIONS-

- NOTES / QUESTIONS-

PERSISTENT AND CONSISTENT

For you to be successful as an owner in the world of Wallstreet, trading shares, market stagnation, market volatility, and all the ups and downs of news cycles, you have to educate yourself and be willing to create a plan to win. Use the list of books outlined in *The Common Man's Financial Guide*, to help you develop your own unique strategy, based on a combination of:

1. Your risk tolerance
2. You time horizon
3. Your current financial position
4. Your financial goals and objectives, and
5. Your ability to be persistent and consistent in your methods and in executing your plan

There have been many times, I failed to follow my established plan and missed some opportunities to increase my ROI, total number of shares, or overall value of my portfolio. People in general are emotionally attached to their money (or lack thereof), and make many key financial decisions based on these emotions. Most times their emotions lead them to make rash and unwise buy or sell decisions as it relates to stocks. After reading *The Common Man's Financial Guide* you will have a better perspective as how to avoid making emotional financial decisions. Your decision to buy, sell, hold a company's stock must be calculated based on historical data, future outlook, popular sentiment, and current execution.

Persistent and Consistent Activity: *Fill in the blanks below with your information.*

1. Set aside a certain percentage of your income for investments each month
2. _____%   Total amount $_____.
3. Set a certain day of the week to check on your investments _____.
4. Set a specific time of day to make trade decisions _____.
5. Set a time to read and educate yourself until you are comfortable with making investment decisions _____.
6. Set a decreased percentage *threshold to buy* stocks on "bad news" _____.
7. Set an increased percentage *threshold to trigger sell* a small percentage of your stocks and preserve profits _____.
8. Review your entire portfolio several times during the year to determine if your plan needs to be adjusted _____. (enter the frequency that you plan to review your plan)

- NOTES / QUESTIONS-

- NOTES / QUESTIONS-

STAY CONNECTED TO THE COMMON MAN'S FINANCIAL GUIDE

1. Download the progressive web app (**App.thecmfg.com**).

2. View past webinars and podcasts on the site.

3. Use the *"Ask Donell"* portal anytime you have a question.

4. Sign up in the VIP section to receive current updates and financial education.

5. Order additional books from the website and save up to 20% off additional purchases. Books are a great gift for family, friends and co-workers.

6. Send the book and/or workbook to friends and family. *(We are not free until we are all free.)*

7. Plan a family financial webinar night on most Thursday nights throughout the year.

8. Stay connected via email: eagledart@aol.com

9. Stay connected via text (303-520-8236). Once you log onto the site you will begin getting updates via texts and emails.

10. Setup a 3-4 hour financial seminar for 10-100 people. Seminars can be scheduled for work groups, religious groups, family groups, civic groups, and social networks.

CONCLUSION

This information is too important to keep to yourself. Please pass it forward to all those you know and associate with. We have to, we need to, or we must change the way we look at money. We must change our relationship with money. I stated this in *The Common Man's Financial Guide*, but it bears repeating: *"Love people, use money!"*

The best and most successful way to get a better relationship with money is to *allow your money to work for you*. There are many vehicles that can be used to let money work, and the vehicle of becoming an owner of 15-20 different successful companies is my passion. Some people love real estate, others like operating different businesses, still others don't mind working for someone else. The one thing we have in common is we all need our money to work for us if we are going to enjoy life to its fullest.

Your financial goals and expertise will help you with the different money-making vehicles, but *The Common Man's Financial Guide* and this workbook were written to help any and all people, no matter where their money comes from.

Don't rush to begin investing, but initially get a thorough understanding and complete, at least this workbook, before getting started. Set up an appointment with a financial planner or advisor (a fiduciary is preferred) to review your current financial situation and create a complete analysis. A fiduciary planner will always place your needs and financial well-being above that of themselves or their company. If you ask them, they are obligated to inform you if that is indeed the case. (Smith, 2019)

- NOTES / QUESTIONS-

Smith II Smith Enterprises, LLC

E. Donell Smith
Personal Financial Consultant/Educator
Eagledart@aol.com
303-520-8236

Author: *Common Man's Financial Guide: Making Money Work for You!*
Progressive Website/App:
App.Thecmfg.com

Yolonda Troupe Smith
Creative Director, SIIS
Preacher/Teacher/Singer/Song Writer/Jingles
Ytroupe@aol.com
601-529-5444
Author: *"The Holy Spirit, The Person, The Works, Don't Live Without Him"*
New Single: *Break Loose* - Available Now!

www.ingramcontent.com/pod-product-compliance
Lightning Source LLC
Chambersburg PA
CBHW051802200326
41597CB00025B/4650